Young Chicago

Joseph Rosa
The Art Institute of Chicago / Yale University Press
A+D SERIES

A+D SERIES

Young Chicago has been published in conjunction with an exhibition of the same title organized by and presented at the Art Institute of Chicago from November 16, 2006, to April 29, 2007.

The exhibition is funded by the Fellows of the Department of Architecture and Design with ongoing support from the Architecture and Design Society.

This is a publication of the Ernest R. Graham Study Center for Architectural Drawing at the Art Institute of Chicago.

First edition
Printed in the United States of America

Library of Congress Control Number:
20066935847
ISBN–13 978–0–300–12067–7
ISBN–10 0–300–12067–2

Published by
The Art Institute of Chicago
111 South Michigan Avenue
Chicago, Illinois 60603–6404
www.artic.edu

Distributed by
Yale University Press
302 Temple Street
P.O. Box 209040
New Haven, Connecticut 06520–9040
www.yalebooks.com

Produced by the Publications Department of the Art Institute of Chicago, Susan F. Rossen, Executive Director
Edited by Robert V. Sharp, Director of Publications
Production by Amanda W. Freymann, Production Specialist
Photography research by Sarah K. Hoadley, Photography Editor
Series design: 2 x 4, New York
Book design by Jeff Wonderland, Associate Director, Department of Graphic Design and Communication Services
Separations by Professional Graphics, Rockford, Illinois
Printing and binding by Lake County Press, Waukegan, Illinois

Photography Credits

Unless otherwise noted, all images are courtesy of the individuals or firms whose work is represented in this catalogue.

Previous book in the A + D Series
Douglas Garofalo (2006)

Contents

Foreword

Since the early twentieth century, Chicago has continually fostered young design talent and established itself as a pivotal center for the arts. To celebrate this historical lineage of design and the twenty-fifth anniversary of the founding of the Art Institute of Chicago's Department of Architecture, Joseph Rosa, John H. Bryan Curator of Architecture and Design, has undertaken this catalogue and the exhibition that it accompanies in which he examines the community's diverse body of contemporary designers and showcases the depth and breadth of the city's creative talents in architecture, industrial design, graphic design, and fashion. In preparing this project, Joseph Rosa has selected sixteen young firms or individuals whose work is not represented in the Art Institute's collection. In the coming year, however, with the assistance of Zoë Ryan, newly named Neville Bryan Curator of Design, works from these studios will become part of the museum's permanent holdings in keeping with the newly expanded mission of the renamed Department of Architecture and Design.

Throughout this project Joseph Rosa was assisted by Michelle Revelt, who researched and wrote the entries for this catalogue; Carissa Kowalski Dougherty, who contributed the artist and studio biographies; Lori Boyer, who coordinated the detailing of each loan; and volunteers Phil Kennedy and Harvey Choldin, who complete this team with their never-ending dedication to the department. In addition, I express my gratitude to the talented designers whose work is featured in this book and exhibition. I would also like to acknowledge members of the Publications Department for their work on the catalogue: Robert V. Sharp, Director; Production Specialist Amanda W. Freymann; and Photography Editor Sarah K. Hoadley. Appreciation goes to Jeff Wonderland, Associate Director of Graphic Design, who skillfully designed this catalogue. The Museum Registration Department under Mary Solt—in particular Tamra Yost, Associate Registrar for Loans and Exhibitions—was invaluable in executing the transportation of exhibition items. Gratitude is extended to our Conservation staff—Doug Severson, Eva-Maria Schuchardt, Lauren Chang, Barbara Korbel, Harriet Stratis, Kristi Dahm, Emily Heye, and Barbara Hall—for giving careful attention to each exhibition object. We are most thankful to John Molini and Craig Cox and the shipping and installation staff of Museum Registration for their care in handling and presenting the works of art, and to Ray Carlson and Bill Foster for their handling of the audiovisual elements in the exhibition. In addition, we acknowledge Curator Christa Thurman and her staff in the Department of Textiles for their help and expertise. We are also grateful to William Caddick and Thomas Barnes, the Executive Director and Associate Director, respectively, of the Department of Physical Plant, and their staff for the care they have given to the exhibition space.

Special appreciation also goes to Carrie Heinonen, Vice President for Marketing and Public Affairs, and Erin Hogan, Director of Public Affairs, for their promotion of the exhibition. I wish to express our gratitude to Executive Director Ray Van Hook and his staff in the Department of Protection Services for their excellence in overseeing all our exhibitions. We are extremely grateful to the Fellows of the Department of Architecture and Design for their vital financial support, as well as the long-standing devotion of the Architecture and Design Society, Karen Hyatt, President. I especially thank Harold Schiff for his unwavering and generous support of the Department of Architecture and Design. Finally, my heartfelt appreciation goes to the staff in the Office of the President and Director: Dorothy Schroeder, Associate Director for Exhibitions and Museum Administration; Jeanne Ladd, Vice President for Museum Finances; and Dawn Koster, Museum Fiscal Affairs Coordinator.

James Cuno
President and Eloise W. Martin Director
The Art Institute of Chicago

BLACK-CROWNED NIGHT HERON

0.60 m

0.54 m

4
A

5
A

0.38 m

STICKS, TWIGS, REEDS

0.71 m

Young Chicago: Contemporary Ideologies by Joseph Rosa

Throughout the twentieth century, Chicago has continually fostered young design talents, establishing itself as a pivotal center for the arts of architecture, industrial design, graphic design, and fashion. The city, however, is best known for and most equated with its built environment. The quality and collective volume of work by such masters as Louis Sullivan, Frank Lloyd Wright, and Ludwig Mies van der Rohe, just to mention a few, is truly astonishing. Their achievements in fact have greatly overshadowed the considerable strides made in industrial and graphic design, as well as the city's contribution to fashion. Furthermore, interest in Chicago's built architecture has continually slighted other, now less well known figures who demonstrated strong conceptual thinking—even with fewer works constructed—or offered ideologies that were too progressive for the already enshrined Chicago School.

While Chicago is known as the city that invented the skyscraper, it was also the first city in America to pioneer prefabricated modern housing—a movement that in recent years has enjoyed an international revival.[1] General Houses, Inc., established by architect and engineer Howard Fisher in 1933, was at the forefront of mass-produced housing methodologies, and by the late 1930s had built numerous dwellings in the Midwest and on the East Coast.[2] A similar trajectory of lost notoriety can be seen in the early, published-but-unbuilt work of the brothers Monroe and Irving Bowman. When Philip Johnson and Henry Russell Hitchcock curated their seminal 1932 international survey show for New York's Museum of Modern Art entitled *Modern Architecture—International Exhibition*, they included only six American studios, two of which represented Chicago: Frank Lloyd Wright and Bowman Brothers (fig. 2).[3] In Johnson and Hitchcock's accompanying exhibition catalogue of the same name, the Bowman brothers were cited as having "as yet built very little but their thorough study of steel construction in relation to architecture...may

Fig. 1 Studio Blue, Ford Calumet Environmental Center, design competition entry (detail), 2004

7

revolutionize certain phases of American architecture within the next few years. Their concern with structural probity and frankness has led them very naturally to work in the International Style."⁴ That same year Johnson and Hitchcock produced a different publication—independent of the exhibition catalogue—entitled *The International Style: Architecture since 1922*. In this now-infamous publication, the minimal modern aesthetic became a pattern book for how to generate designs that adhered to the principles of the movement. To make matters—as well as its history—even more confusing, Johnson and Hitchcock revised their selection of works from the exhibition for this second book and elimi-

Fig. 2 Bowman Brothers, Project for the Lux Apartments, Evanston, Illinois, 1931. From *Modern Architecture—International Exhibition* (Museum of Modern Art, 1932), p. 177.

nated architects who either did not securely fit their International Style framework or simply had not realized their own modernist designs. In the process both Wright (for ideological differences) and the Bowman Brothers (because their work was not yet built) fell from grace and were omitted from this influential publication. Hence the role of Chicago as a leading voice in modern architecture was for a time silenced.

In an interview decades later, Philip Johnson reflected on his treatment of the Bowman brothers: "I was more impressed by their ideas than their built works."⁵ Yet, while the Bowmans' work diminished in international scale in the 1930s, other studios grew to prominence. George Fred Keck's designs, for example, became more modern in character, as did the oeuvre of Bertrand Goldberg—one of the few Americans to study at the Bauhaus and one who worked for Mies van der Rohe in Germany before returning to his hometown of Chicago.[6] Mies's own emigration from Germany in 1938 to teach at the Armour Institute (later to become the Illinois Institute of Technology) officially marked the arrival in Chicago of the International Style, and with it an ideology of Cartesian boxes became the city's avant-garde.[7]

Since the advent of the International Style, numerous others who have promulgated different ideologies have contributed to the city's legacy.[8] While many have furthered the methodology of Mies's teachings, those who have provided additional avant-garde vocabularies include Walter Netsch, Stanley Tigerman, and Helmut Jahn, as well as Ron Krueck and Mark Sexton, Doug Garofalo, and Jeanne Gang. They have all helped foster the legacy of progressive ideology that is synonymous with Chicago's history. The city has always benefited from this synergy by allowing the younger, cutting-edge studios to operate concurrently with larger and more established ones.

While its architectural fabric can easily personify a city, the disciplines of industrial design, graphic design, and fashion are equated with larger cultural productions and ideologies that are national in scale. Hence, these disciplines are not associated with a particular city or a region, with the exception of their impact on local economies. Since the early 1920s, industrial design has played a significant role in Chicago.[9] The first company to mass-produce a line of tubular metal furniture in America was the W. H. Howell Company, which opened in the city in 1929 and went on to market other definitive designs by local architects in the 1930s that epitomized the International Style. By mid-century Chicago was the home office of such companies as Montgomery Ward and Company; Sunbeam; Sears, Roebuck and Company; and Motorola—all of which were producing industrial design objects that became powerhouses of brand image. While some of these businesses had their own in-house design studios—as Ann Swainson did for Montgomery Ward—others brought in nationally known names such as Henry Dreyfuss to design objects for the market.[10]

A significant factor in the quality of industrial and graphic design in Chicago was the pedagogical framework at the New Bauhaus, established in 1937 under the direction of László Moholy-Nagy, who, like Mies, had been a faculty member of the Bauhaus in Weimar, Germany. Moholy's New Bauhaus lasted only a year; his second attempt, the School of Design, founded in 1939, fared better; in 1944 it was renamed the Institute of Design.[11] The influence of the radically avant-garde Bauhaus ideology was kept alive in the city by both Moholy-Nagy and György Kepes, yet another teacher from the original Bauhaus. Their Bauhaus colleague Herbert Bayer—an Austrian-born graphic designer working in New York City—also became a consultant for the Chicago-based Container Corporation of America. Interest in typography and logo branding grew in Chicago post–World War II and had tremendous impact on the development of corporate identities. This breadth can be seen in the diversity of output: from the 1953 Playboy logo designed by Arthur Paul—a symbol of Hugh Hefner's empire—to the iconic 1965 Minute Maid label created by Sid Dickens.[12]

The realm of fashion remains the most underexplored of these disciplines in Chicago, despite the fact that one of the first fashion departments in the country was established at the School of the Art Institute of Chicago in 1934. At the time of its inception, the department took as its mission the formation of young couturiers; today this is still essential to the school's pedagogy. This influence can be seen in the ideology and career trajectory of designer/artist J. Morgan Puett, a 1981 BFA graduate of the School who majored in sculpture and experimental filmmaking. Early in her career she became known in New York for elegant minimal dresses that were beautifully assembled art objects. Shortly thereafter she shifted direction and closed her commercial storefront to become an artist who uses the culture of clothing as her subject matter. Puett started designing site-specific art installations that are metanarratives for the context and culture of clothing.

To celebrate the remarkable lineage of design in Chicago and the twenty-fifth anniversary of the founding of the museum's Department of Architecture, this catalogue and the exhibition it accompanies look at the community's rich diversity of contemporary designers and feature the city's ever-growing talents in architecture, industrial design, graphic design, and fashion. The studios selected represent a small sampling of the ideologies—from digital literacy and conceptual methodologies to contextualism, brand legacy, and cultural identity—that are global in scope and emblematic of a twenty-first-century Chicago.

ARCHITECTURE

The 2006 design of a museum for prehistoric archaeology, created for the Jeongok-ri site in Gyeonggi-do, Korea, is an example of the kind of digital literacy that can be found in today's avant-garde studios. Paul Preissner, principal of the studio Qua'Virarch, took cues from the site's undulating terrain to generate a design solution that is a metanarrative of the landscape. From a distance the vast structure appears to be a visual extension of the landscape; on closer examination, however, this complex, ethereal building reveals itself. This sense of fluidity in the building's overall massing is also employed in its program through walkways, stairs, and elevators that provide a contiguous network of circulation. Through digital conception and fabrication, the structure of this building would be a series of concrete beams and columns that are woven together for rigidity to create a lattice for this undulating form and to provide visual transparencies through the building's exterior, admitting natural light deep into interior public spaces.

The use of digital methodologies in emerging studios has allowed contemporary architecture to become truly contextual to its site and program. This can be seen most immediately in the formal manipulation of new building shapes, but it is also manifested in the use of informal data to generate an architectural form. This methodology is beautifully illustrated by UrbanLab's 2001 proposal for a Visitor Information Center for the City of Chicago. Principals Sarah Dunn and Martin Felsen took an existing structure on Randolph Street just west of Michigan Avenue and created a dynamic visitors' center. Showcasing the studio's diverse talents—in architecture and urban design—they created a space that made the building's interior a microcosm of the greater Chicago area. In their hands the space inside is transformed into a diorama with a ramp that ascends the perimeter walls so that visitors can view photographic murals of notable buildings in the city and get an elevated perspective on a map of Chicago that occupies the structure's vast floor. But the notion of a diorama takes on a new interpretation at the building's bulging street façade, which becomes a viewing platform onto the city. To achieve this façade, the architects elegantly folded and bent the glass curtain wall in a variety of angles, thereby directing the attention of individuals inside toward views of actual buildings in the landscape.

Contrary to the general misconception that digital literacy will digress into gratuitous form making, it has actually provided architects, landscape designers, and urban planners with the tools—and intellectual discourse—to explore further their respective disciplines, question their boundaries, and chart new territory. This has resulted in refreshing solutions for rethinking cities, solutions that build on the existing urban fabric to generate new ideas that are contextual and can be implemented over time. Clare Lyster Studio's 2006 speculative project for a neighborhood in Chicago—entitled *Lawndale: Expanding the Latent Landscape*—is a perfect example of this type of thinking. Through research, writing, and design, Lyster explores the production of public space at the apex of building, landscape, and infrastructure. For *Lawndale* Lyster produced a framework that included redefining land use, investigating the value of land swaps, and constructing a landscaped infrastructure that would become the matrix for a stable, long-term, planned reconfiguration of the neighborhood.

Fig. 3 Avram Lothan, DeStefano + Partners, Lothan House, Chicago, 2005

The 2003 Intergenerational Learning Center by 3D Design Studio provides a new contextual typology for the aged. By fusing together the notion of an institutional facility and the spatial characteristics of domestic residential living, Darryl Crosby and Melinda Palmore—principals of 3D Design Studio—produced a building for transitional living that reestablished the context of its urban fabric. Formally, this is achieved by a series of residential houses that demarcate one end of the site and proportionally fit into the domestic fabric. Perpendicular to this row of houses is a more dynamic, free-form structure somewhat more public in scale and reminiscent of a large community library. But it is the misinterpretation of the scale of these buildings and the physical spaces between these two visual typologies that allows the Intergenerational Learning Center to chart new formal directions. The customary hierarchy of residential buildings is here flipped: the front yard is actually the back and the backyard is an internal private circulation corridor that takes you to the reception area of the public building. Within this public structure are facilities for residents, as well as for the staff, that make this transitional Learning Center both a civilized setting and an aesthetically progressive model that fits into the domestic scale of Chicago's urban fabric.

Historically, constraints on domestic architecture in urban settings have produced some of the most innovative design solutions. Avram Lothan's 2005 Lothan House in Lincoln Park (fig. 3) is a prime example of pushing the envelope in a historical and contextual setting. Lothan—a principal with DeStefano + Partners—employed a U-shaped courtyard typology in this brick-clad Victorian neighborhood. To contextualize this modern massing, the three-story house is sheathed in brick with metal cladding at the second floor. Seen from the outside the house fits into the street roofline, but once inside, one discovers an exterior courtyard adjacent to the two-story living room. Inside this minimalist interior a sense of tactility is achieved through woods and metals that are employed as surfaces and screens. Lothan's design is an example of how the courtyard typology can be redefined and situated successfully in today's historical urban fabric.

The redefinition of typologies and normative notions of architectural character can also be seen in the work of John Ronan, whose 2004 design for the Perth Amboy High School in New Jersey blurs the boundaries between the institution and the community it serves. Formally, Ronan superimposed three conceptual systems defined as the Mat (the site), the Barscape (the academic facilities), and the Tower—all three of which are communally programmed spaces shared with the neighborhood and that collectively make up the landscape of this vast high school. Compositionally, it is an elegant solution with visual nodes—the Towers—that reach out into the community as spaces for public events. Ronan's notion of the Mat and the Barscape also provides a cohesive urban fabric for an institutional facility inserted into the existing landscape. His design is an elegant solution that encodes new formal relationships and rethinks the role of institutions in the greater community.

While Chicago and its architectural community are known for having invented the skyscraper, this building typology has expanded around the world into a visual repertoire of formal iterations. The 2006 Infinity Tower—a residential structure designed by Ross Wimer of Skidmore, Owings & Merrill, Chicago, for Dubai, United Arab Emirates—will be a welcome addition to this historical lexicon and another first for a Chicago architectural office: the world's tallest 90-degree spiral building. The building's projected completion date is 2009. To achieve this rotated form, Wimer turns each floor plate—which is the same size throughout the structure—just 1.2 degrees around the building's central core, thereby creating an elegant and fluid form. Wimer's visually spiraling tower is emblematic of a generation of younger designers who are committed to furthering the notion of tall buildings and the means by which they can be achieved in the twenty-first century.

Jordan Mozer's 2005 design for the hotel East, located in Hamburg, Germany, is a perfect example of his ability to create event spaces within existing conditions, for he took an abandoned factory building and with some new adjacent construction created a vast complex that houses a hotel, restaurants, bars, and a lounge—all of which showcase his unique hyperorganic forms. The interior surfaces and furnishings are custom designs by Mozer and his studio, and they demonstrate how Mozer creates a visual narrative that unifies disparate spaces into one cohesive experience. The main dining room of the restaurant, with its 35-foot-high ceilings, exemplifies this: Mozer inserted large, white, undulating faux columns intermittently in the space to further express its verticality. The formal character of the fluted, undulating lines of the columns is reiterated—at a smaller scale—throughout the complex, from the dining chairs to the bedroom suites.

INDUSTRIAL DESIGN

One of the most important and influential tastemakers in the United States, Holly Hunt established her furniture company in Chicago in 1984. Ten years later she launched a line of furniture by the haute-couture French interior designer Christian Liaigre—already famous for his custom furnishings—and made his work accessible for the mass-produced luxury market. To the industry this move clearly illustrated that Hunt was a visionary business woman who also knew style. Little more than a decade later the Holly Hunt Collection has expanded beyond furniture and lighting to include leather and textiles. The company carries the exclusive line by Liaigre, as well as designs by John Hutton and Kevin Reilly. Holly Hunt also has seven showrooms throughout the United States that showcase these collections and work by other designers.

The Holly Hunt signature look is epitomized by furniture pieces of dark woods and opulent, neutral-colored fabrics and by light fixtures that are spare, minimal, and elegant in character—objects that collectively connote an aesthetic of modern luxury. Hunt's design for the South Beach Chair—from her 2004 Studio H Collection—illustrates her ability to rethink styles and create a fresh, clean, contemporary design aesthetic. The curved upholstered back of the South Beach Chair is separated from the seat cushion by an narrowly proportioned horizontal opening that visually reduces the lower half of the chair's mass as it descends to its streamlined wooded legs.

Motorola, an internationally respected brand name, is actually a Chicago company established in 1928. Long regarded for its quality television sets, Motorola has today become synonymous with cellular telephones and other electronic devices. Building on Motorola's brand legacy over the years, the company has reconceived its products and its approach to prevailing demographics to become a leading figure in the mobile industry, while also expanding into other arenas as illustrated by their partnership with Burton Snowboards to produce the 2006 Audex jacket, each with an MP3 player created by Motorola. Its industrial design studio under the direction of Peter Pfanner brings together designers from all over the world. This diversity of talent—and their brand demographics—is also reflected in the narratives for their mobile designs. As cellular telephone technology becomes ever more ubiquitous in today's culture, it is essential that the design of these phones take on characteristics that enable them to communicate the metanarrative of the user and the user's cultural demographics. Motorola's phones are not just functional objects: they embody and express character. The 2006 RAZR is the slimmest phone on the market and its name plays off its striking profile, while the more bulbous 2006 PEBL offers an object as exquisite as a waterworn stone carried home from the shore.

At the other end of the industrial design spectrum is IDEO—a design studio founded in 1991 by David Kelly in Palo Alto, California. While the IDEO name never appears on objects the firm produces, a remarkable number of aesthetically progressive designs on the market today have been shaped and refined by IDEO. Today the firm has studios in London, Munich, and Shanghai, as well as the U.S. Their Chicago studio was established in 1991 by Craig Sampson; in 1995 Martin Thaler dissolved his own creative studio to become design director. Located in Evanston, this office is staffed by a host of industrial designers who are producing objects that showcase technologies coupled with aesthetics: in short, beautiful objects functionally conceived. This can be seen in the range of their work from the 2004 LifePort Kidney Transporter to the 2005 inMotion iM7—a desktop audio system intended for an iPod.

IDEO's prototype for the LifePort Kidney Transporter was conceived in conjunction with Organ Recovery Systems. The development of a highly compact mechanical configuration—that continually monitors the viability of the kidney during transport—allowed the container to maintain its manageable size. The inMotion iM7 contains a speaker system and a dock for an iPod. The sleek, cylindrical, perforated form conceals the audio components, while cradling the iPod in its own niche.

GRAPHIC DESIGN

Studio Blue builds on the history of classic twentieth-century modern graphic design to generate an aesthetic sensibility and methodology that is uniquely theirs. The work of partners Cheryl Towler Weese and Kathy Fredrickson evokes design narratives that embody the characteristics of their subject matter; hence, no two projects are the same. Their 2003 brand identity and catalogue design for Otis College of Art and Design, located in Los Angeles, California, is a perfect example of their ideology. The result is a visual ensemble of graphic identities for each of the school's departments that when reassembled in the catalogue reflects the breadth of the institution's mission. Weese and Fredrickson created graphic identities from patterns or creative processes that reflect the craft of making. The physical act of drawing, for example—the creation of a line or marking on a surface—becomes a graphic element that moves across a page in the catalogue from which the department name Fine Arts emerges. Studio Blue's sense of playfulness and metanarrative constructions can also be seen in their 2004 entry for the Ford Calumet Environmental Center poster design competition (fig. 1). Picking up on the words *environmental* and *design*, they produced a poster that connotes these terms. At first glance one sees in the foreground a tree, a black-crowned night heron, and the heron's nest. In the background there rises the silhouette of a grain silo. On closer viewing, however, one sees that the bird's nest is completely measured out with dimensions—rendering the poster an architectural construction drawing.

The exuberant work of JNL Graphic Design's principal Jason Pickleman results in designs that play with visual gestures more influenced by the praxis of modern and contemporary art than the more normative historical practice of graphic design. His rejection of the past allows Pickleman to generate newfound relationships not traditionally associated with printed matter. This is evident in his 2003 CD packaging for the Aluminum Group, for which composites of multiple exposures of faces compose the front and back cover images. The CD packaging also reflects early avant-garde art practices. The multiple exposures of the faces signify aspects of simultaneity that are found in Marcel Duchamp's early Cubist works and early Surrealist photography by Man Ray.

Pickleman's work also visually plays with antiquated and idealized notions of printing production methods that predate the use of computers in graphic design studios: witness his 2005 printed matter—menu, check card, letterhead, and business card—for Avec, a restaurant in Chicago's Warehouse District. Here all outer surfaces of the printed matter are covered with text in a type font generated from an old typewriter or letterpress printing. This text, however, is deleted by lines that run through it, creating a strong, horizontally banded surface. Only one line in each of these printed pieces stops to reveal the name of the restaurant in a new bold lowercase font: avec.

The work of Roy Brooks, principal of the graphic design studio Fold Four, subverts traditional typologies in printed matter to produce refreshing solutions that engage the reader. This is evident with his 2005 brochure for a Rob Fischer exhibition at the Whitney Museum of American Art. The front, back, and side flaps of the brochure are wrapped with images of the artist's work. Inserted into this—like a signature in a book—is the extended brochure text. The dense layout of the text is graphically addressed as if it were a book with endnotes appearing vertically in the gutter of each spread. Each paragraph is slightly off the two-column template for the page—a nod to the aesthetic of the artist's work. The resulting brochure appears to be more akin to a design structure for a book on the artist. Brooks's design ideology plays off the narrative of the artist—or subject matter—and resituates the medium in which it will be expressed. Graphically, Brooks's booklike brochure on Fischer looks very different from his 2005 design for an Andrea Zittel invitation. The invitation is a simple, horizontal, folded card with a minimal amount of text on the cover and no image. Yet, once opened, the piece presents an image spanning the length of the invitation and revealing an aesthetic and visual setting equated with Zittel's subject matter, the desert.

FASHION

The fashion industry's model for avant-garde ideology was radically revised when legendary French couture house Christian Dior hired John Galliano as its new designer in 1997. Galliano's runway shows became visual spectacles informed by complex narratives that questioned identity and drew inspiration from history and art, making the event a cultural filter for larger social issues. The *Soundsuits* of fashion designer and artist Nick Cave also fit into an avant-garde trajectory by questioning issues of social identity and history through fashion. Cave's *Soundsuits*, which must also be heard to be understood, engage the notion of physical movement as expressed in runway shows. Many of Cave's designs have covered or extended head pieces, among them, his 2006 *Soundsuit*, to which he gave a silhouette that references the infamous pointed hood of the Ku Klux Klan. This chevron form is a contiguous fabric surface that extends from the garment's shoulders and rises over three feet in height. In Cave's work this familiar symbol of cultural oppression, however, is adorned with hand beading and other objects and becomes an integral element of the *Soundsuit*, thereby allowing his own histories—as a black male and a fashion designer—to become metanarratives for his own creations.

The act of couture—the physical making of clothing—can also be seen in the work of fashion designer and artist Cat Chow. Chow's sculptural designs rely on found objects such as zippers or tape measures that she transforms into the foundations of her work. Most pieces contain one type of found object employed by her in a serial-like manner to produce a monolithic design. Chow's 2003 *Hourglass* is an example of her experimentation with one single-length zipper to produce a design for a skirt that is installed on a wall surface and connected by a zipper to another similar form that hangs off the wall. While this piece is one of her unwearable creations, it is a critical work in the development of her methodology as a designer, a methodology that emerges through her sense of tactility and invention and that is evident in all of her wearable designs.

Notes

1. Allison Arieff and Bryan Burkhart, *Prefab* (Gibbs Smith, 2002).

2. For more on prefabricated housing in America, see F. R. S. Yorke, *The Modern House* (Architectural Press, 1934); Allan D. Wallis, *Wheel Estates: The Rise and Decline of Mobile Homes* (Oxford University Press, 1991); H. Ward Jandl, *Yesterday's Houses of Tomorrow: Innovative American Homes, 1850 to 1950* (Preservation Press, 1991).

3. For more on the history of the exhibition, see Terence Riley, *The International Style: Exhibition 15 and The Museum of Modern Art* (Rizzoli International/Columbia Books of Architecture, 1992).

4. *Modern Architecture — International Exhibition* (Museum of Modern Art, 1932), p.16.

5. Joseph Rosa interview with Philip Johnson, May 28, 1987.

6. For more on Keck, see Robert Boyce, *Keck and Keck* (Princeton Architectural Press, 1993); and on Goldberg, see Paul Heyer, *American Architecture: Ideas and Ideologies in the Late Twentieth Century* (Wiley, 1993); Michel Ragon, *Goldberg: Dans la Ville/Goldberg: On the City* (Paris Art Center, 1985); Margret Kentgens-Craig, *The Bauhaus and America: First Contacts, 1919–1936* (1999; rpt. MIT Press, 2001); Geoffrey Goldberg, "Bertrand Goldberg: A Personal View of Architecture," and Katerina Rüedi Ray, "Making Marina City: Men, Money, Masquerade and Modernity," in *Chicago Architecture: Histories, Revisions, Alternatives*, edited by Charles Waldheim and Katerina Rüedi Ray (University of Chicago Press, 2005).

7. For more on the influence of Mies on American architecture and the Chicago scene, see Phyllis Lambert, ed., *Mies in America* (Canadian Centre for Architecture/Whitney Museum of American Art/Harry N. Abrams, 2001); Franz Schulze, "Mies van der Rohe in America," in *Chicago Architecture and Design, 1923–1993: Reconfiguration of an American Metropolis*, edited by John Zukowsky (Art Institute of Chicago/Prestel-Verlag, 1993), pp. 141–57; Detlef Mertins, ed., *The Presence of Mies* (Princeton Architectural Press, 1994).

8. For more on this period, see Stuart E. Cohen, *Chicago Architects* (Swallow Press, 1976).

9. For more on industrial design in America and Chicago, see Arthur J. Pulos, *The American Design Adventure, 1940–1975* (MIT Press, 1988).

10. For more on Chicago's role in industrial design, see Pauline Saliga, "'To Build a Better Mousetrap': Design in Chicago, 1920-1970," in *Chicago Architecture and Design* (note 7), pp. 265–81.

11. For more on the history of graphic design in America, see R. Rogers Remington, *American Modernism: Graphic Design 1920–1960* (Yale University Press, 2003); Kentgens-Craig (note 6).

12. For more on graphic design in Chicago, see Victor Margolin, "Graphic Design in Chicago," in *Chicago Architecture and Design* (note 7), pp. 283–301.

Studios

Qua'Virarch

Gyeonggi-do Jeongok Prehistory Museum, Korea, 2006

Since its discovery in 1978, the Jeongok-ri site in Gyeonggi-do, Korea, has become an invaluable resource in the scientific study of human evolution. Although still under excavation, this world-renowned Paleolithic site has already developed into a major center for research. In 2005 the Organizing Committee for the Gyeonggi-do Jeongok Prehistory Museum announced an international design competition that would reflect the importance of this region. Paul Preissner, principal of Qua'Virarch and winner of the competition's second-place prize, envisioned the project as a spatial continuation of the landscape and its organic metamorphosis into a building. In Preissner's proposal, guests access the museum through gardens that extend into the entry to create an inviting transitional area. The heart of the building is the triple-height space of the reception hall, which serves as the main artery for visitor circulation. An interconnected terracing of exhibition spaces includes a gallery for viewing archaeological artifacts and other rooms for studying life during prehistoric eras. By separating each of these spaces with only the circulation platforms, the architect has eliminated visual obstructions and achieved a unified interior. Stone artifacts can be viewed in a continuum of human development, released from static compartmentalization. Panoramic views of the interior also extend into the park and archaeological site.

Devoted to site preservation, Preissner's design also sets new standards in environmental awareness. By utilizing various recycled and recyclable materials and tapping into available sources of natural energy (principally through skylights and photovoltaic roof panels), the structure would approach zero in its net energy consumption.

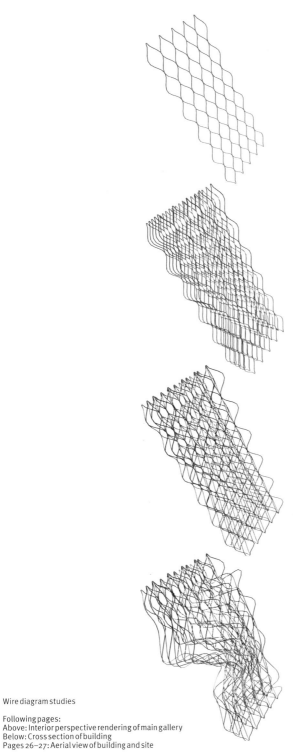

Wire diagram studies

Following pages:
Above: Interior perspective rendering of main gallery
Below: Cross section of building
Pages 26–27: Aerial view of building and site

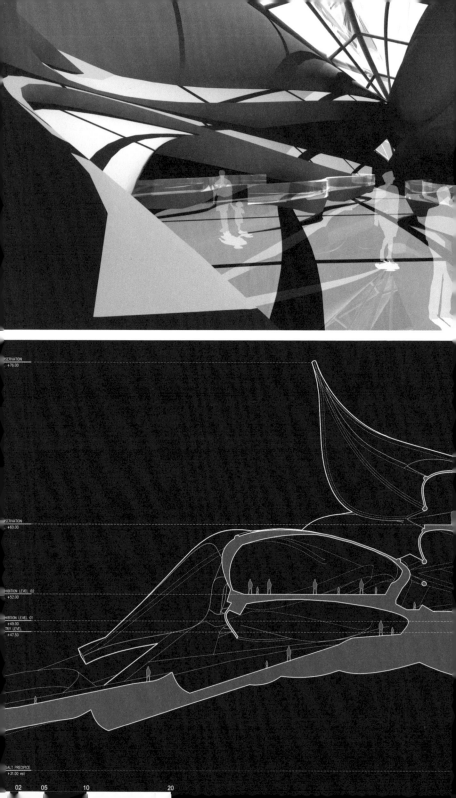

SERVATION
+76.00

SERVATION
+60.00

HIBITION LEVEL 02
+52.00

HIBITION LEVEL 01
+49.00
TRY LEVEL
+47.50

SALT PRECIPICE
+31.00 est

02   05   10   20

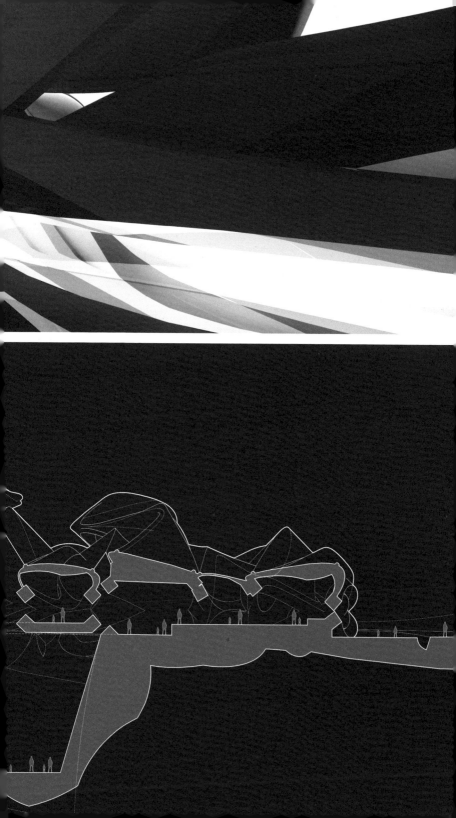

UrbanLab

Visitor Information Center, Chicago, 2001

Architects Sarah Dunn and Martin Felsen suggest that public buildings and public spaces should directly reflect prevailing technology. They see the omnipresent flow of data and information as the most radical force affecting urban living and altering the forms of contemporary architecture. For the City of Chicago's Visitor Information Center—an invitational competition held in 2001—the team envisioned a convergence of information, in both form and purpose. Computer-aided technology played an essential role in their conception of the building, while the center itself would offer tourists an interactive exchange of local and city information.

UrbanLab planned to utilize a computer-integrated manufacturing system to design and fabricate the space-frame and surface cladding. Lighting for the exterior and interior surfaces is contained within the space-frame; its appearance is altered by contextual cues. The dynamic surface of the exterior façade represents three local factors—weather, noise, and events—in a montage of information-based color, turning a cool blue or violet in intense sunlight, or bright yellow to orange red on a cloudy day. The façade can also become saturated in a bright red hue when monitoring the high-decibel roar of an elevated train or take on a different character in response to music played in nearby Millennium Park. Inside, a ramp—composed of structural glass planks on a steel frame—enables visitors to sample a timeline of important events in the history of Chicago. While obtaining maps and pamphlets, guests can orient themselves by means of the main-floor map of Chicago, or watch an informational LED display of events across the city.

Perspective view of building façade

Cutaway perspective view

Following pages:
Interior perspective rendering

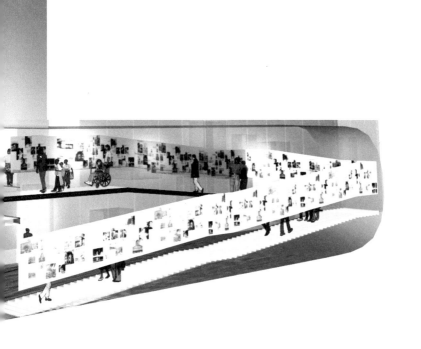

Clare Lyster Studio

Lawndale: Expanding the Latent Landscape (Speculative Project), Chicago, 2006

The economic, political, and social decline of inner-city neighborhoods has long been prevalent in American metropolitan areas, with abundant, vacant postindustrial lots. Realizing the deficiencies of traditional architecture and postwar development proposals, civic leaders and designers have begun to embrace landscape as a vehicle for change. Through her work Clare Lyster suggests that landscape programming can be a short-term solution providing the foundation for further urban development. In *Lawndale: Expanding the Latent Landscape,* Lyster recommends a three-tiered revitalization plan for Chicago's North Lawndale neighborhood on the West Side.

First, privately owned real estate within a central area would be traded for government-owned property in an outlying region of the neighborhood. By acquiring bulk property within this "middle zone," local government could encourage civic development in areas adjacent to the elevated-train stations. Second, once a large quantity of contiguous real estate is amassed, land use will be defined by its proximity to existing transportation and freight infrastructures. For example, an area may be assigned to agricultural development, such as tree farming, and these new facilities will be managed by city and local groups with job-training incentives for area youths. These are but short-term solutions, however: the long-term answer will depend upon permanent businesses flourishing within the newly renewed infrastructure. Finally, located near a residence once occupied by Dr. Martin Luther King, Jr., a new public square called King Park will be established to anchor the community as a cultural center.

Top: Existing urban fabric
Above: View of North Lawndale neighborhood, Chicago

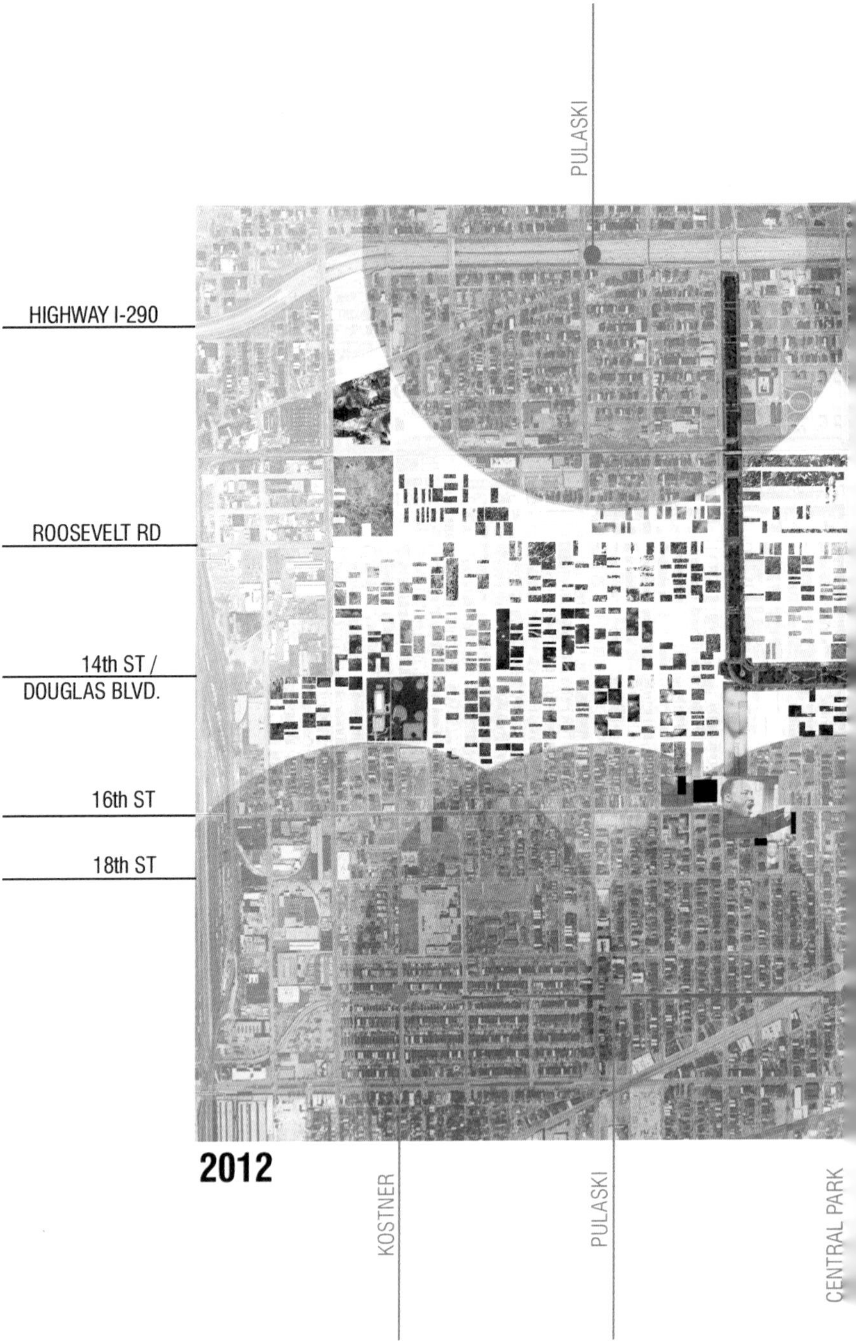

HIGHWAY I-290

ROOSEVELT RD

14th ST /
DOUGLAS BLVD.

16th ST

18th ST

PULASKI

2012

KOSTNER

PULASKI

CENTRAL PARK

Land use analysis, projected for 2012

OGDEN AVE

KEDZIE

CALIFORNIA

WESTERN

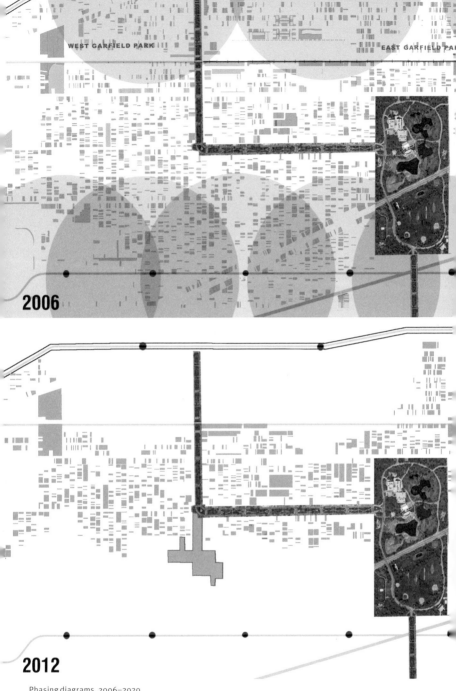

WEST GARFIELD PARK EAST GARFIELD PAR

2006

2012

Phasing diagrams, 2006–2020

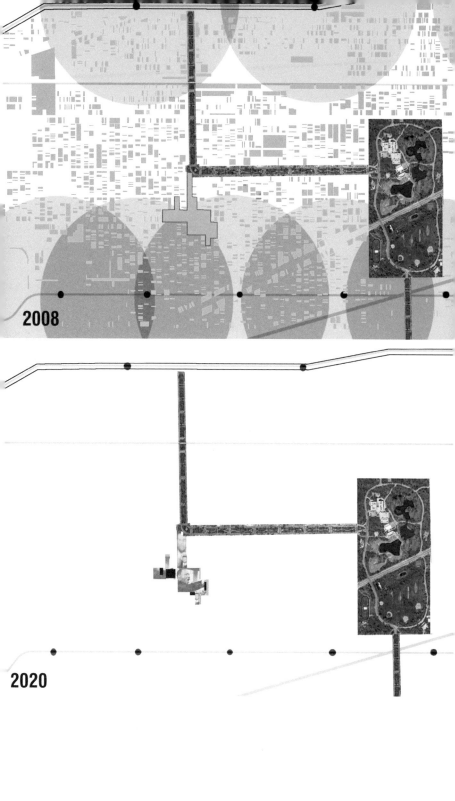

2008

2020

3D Design Studio

Intergenerational Learning Center, Chicago, 2003

As a part of the New Public Works program underwritten by the National Endowment for the Arts, the City of Chicago held a national design competition for a housing and social services center for grandparents who have custody of their grandchildren. The competition entry by Darryl Crosby and Melinda Palmore of 3D Design Studio proposed an Intergenerational Learning Center to provide housing, educational opportunities, and daycare for children and seniors on the South Side.

In 3D Design's proposal, intergenerational, nontraditional families are housed in residences that have the appearance of town houses, but are in fact a single mass of duplex apartments. While the façade of the residential portion faces 104th Street, its main entrance is located on South Michigan Avenue in an oval structure that also provides entry to the Intergenerational Center and its communal functions, principally a senior center and a Head Start program. Considered the heart of the entire complex, this facility is designed with interconnected areas to encourage interaction between the generations. Beyond the large reception lobby, the senior center offers a diner for casual meals and socializing, a floating library, and a fitness center, as well as a movie theater for both television viewing and film nights. In addition to classrooms, the Head Start space contains a gross-motor room with a high clerestory window, from which staff and parents can easily monitor the children.

Photograph of model

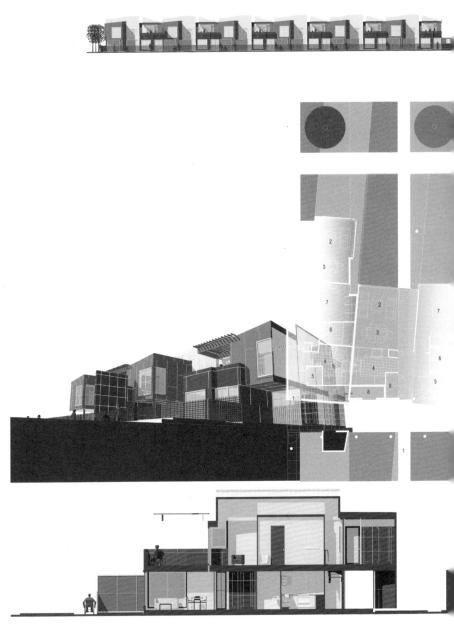

Top: Street elevation of residential complex
Middle: Cutaway perspective view of a unit and plan
Bottom: Cross section through a unit

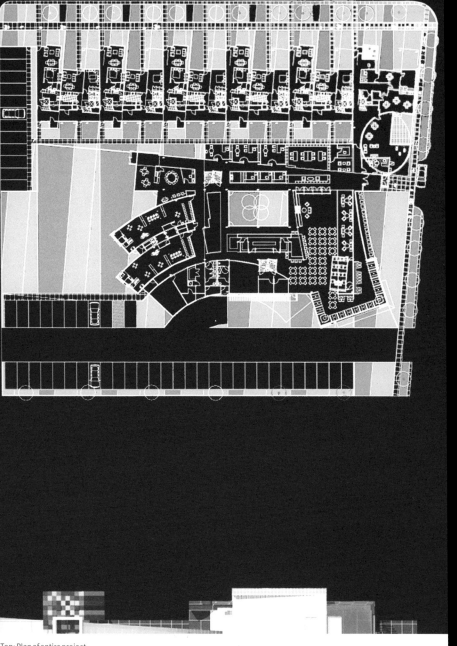

Top: Plan of entire project
Bottom: Elevation

Avram Lothan, DeStefano + Partners

Lothan House, Chicago, 2005

As a design principal at DeStefano + Partners, Avram Lothan embraces the firm's methodology of urban planning, which espouses an unwavering respect for context and the broader public realm. This tenet is tangibly defined in the 2005 Lothan House in Lincoln Park.

Located in a neighborhood of predominantly late-nineteenth-century houses, the Lothan House is a creative, contemporary design solution that melds historic domestic architecture with urban revitalization. On the exterior, the brick home blends seamlessly into a streetscape of distinctly Victorian character, concealing the flair of its thoroughly modern interior. Visitors are greeted in the first-floor foyer, which is flanked by a study. Past the foyer, a two-story living room offers a view of and access to an adjacent outdoor courtyard extending the entire length of the room. This courtyard is carved out of the building's massing, which creates the home's U-shape, while maintaining the rigid boundaries of the rectangular lot. In a departure from tradition, the laundry facility and family room are placed on the second floor, accompanied by the master bedroom and bath. The third floor contains a second bedroom and bath, offering ideal accommodations for houseguests.

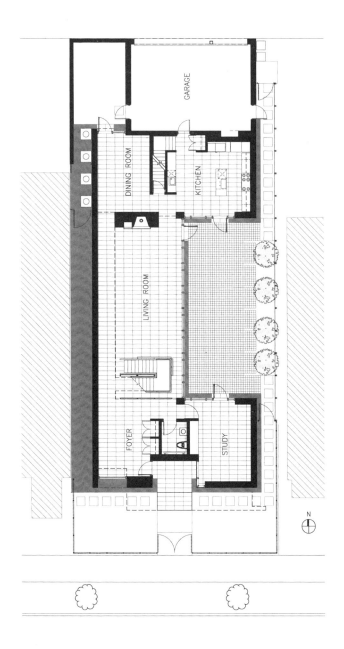

GARAGE

DINING ROOM

KITCHEN

LIVING ROOM

FOYER

STUDY

N

First-floor plan of house

View of living room

View of courtyard

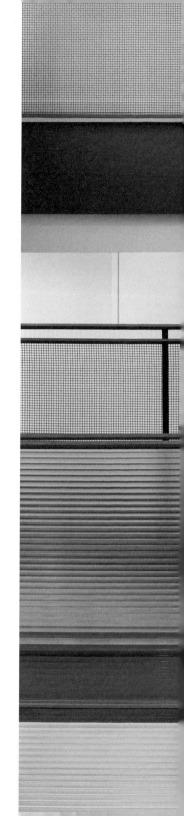

View of staircase

John Ronan Architect

Perth Amboy High School, New Jersey, 2004–

In 2004 the New Jersey Schools Construction Corporation conducted an international competition for Perth Amboy High School. The project called for six learning academies for 3,000 students, as well as a dining venue, performing arts theater, media center, administrative offices, and athletic and support facilities—all on a 15.5-acre site. The project budget totaled $99 million. John Ronan won the competition with an innovative hybrid, a 472,000-square-foot design in which he fused the needs of the school with those of a civic cultural center. His effort to foster unity between the community and its institutions was the impetus behind this winning design.

Ronan based his structure on three component systems that he dubbed the Mat, the Barscape, and the Towers—each distinct in function and visual appearance. The Mat is a continuous surface with designated zones for school and community activities, such as athletics, outdoor learning, and parking; it is composed of various materials, such as grass, rubber, clay, and gravel. Academic areas are located within the Barscape, a community of interconnected "bars." The design of the Barscape allows for flexible arrangements of interior spaces as well as for future expansion to accommodate changing academic needs. In juxtaposition to the horizontal Barscape, the striking, vertical, glass Towers house student and community activity spaces—such as the performing arts theater, media center, and workout facilities. The Towers were conceived as a visual landmark for the community, encouraging civic participation in the life of the school.

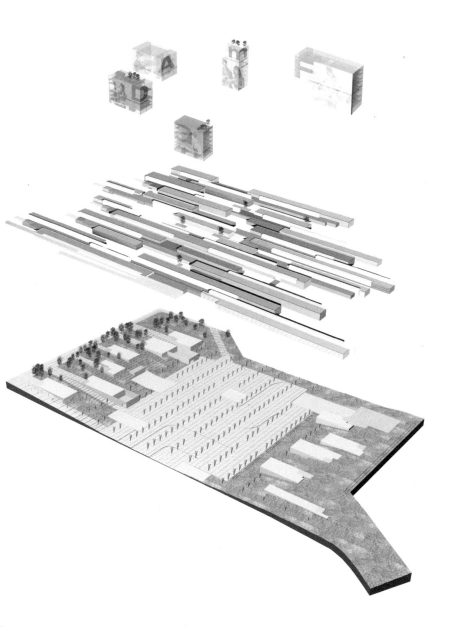

Exploded axonometric rendering of site and building

Following pages:
Above left: Site plan
Below left: Perspective rendering of campus
Above right: Perspective view toward auditorium
Below left: Perspective view toward fitness center

Lite P1

auditorium

Cutaway perspective rendering of entrance to dining hall

Ross B. Wimer,
Skidmore, Owings & Merrill

Infinity Tower, Dubai Marina, United Arab Emirates, 2006–

Designed for the Dubai Marina in United Arab Emirates, the Infinity Tower is a residential building soaring 73 stories and topping out at 306 meters (1,004 feet). Upon its completion in 2009, the Infinity Tower will be the world's tallest building with a 90-degree spiral. The visual impact of Ross B. Wimer's design stems from the gradual rotation of the structural mass around the vertical axis, as the building rises from base to apex. This helix utilizes the building's central elevator core as its axis: each floor of the tower rotates clockwise 1.2 degrees, completing its 90-degree twist at the very top, while maintaining a constant floor plate throughout its height. Already celebrated as a masterpiece of spiraling design, the tower is constructed with high-strength, cast-in-place concrete columns.

The residential structure comprises one-, two-, three-, and four-bedroom apartments, as well as eleven floors of lofts, and three of penthouses. In each unit, an open plan complements the floor-to-ceiling windows and contemporary interior design. Residents will have access to sweeping views of the Arabian Gulf, Palm Island, or the Dubai Marina. The building's amenities include a luxury spa, children's nursery, gymnasium, and conference room facility, as well as retail outlets, outdoor swimming pools, and tennis courts.

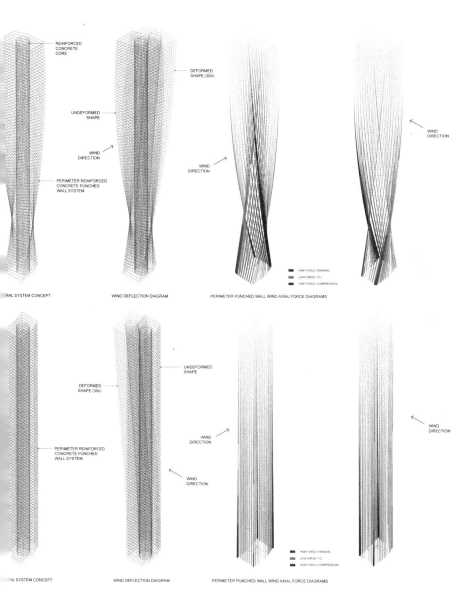

RAL SYSTEM CONCEPT   WIND DEFLECTION DIAGRAM   PERIMETER PUNCHED WALL WIND AXIAL FORCE DIAGRAMS

REINFORCED
CONCRETE
CORE

UNDEFORMED
SHAPE

DEFORMED
SHAPE (30X)

WIND
DIRECTION

WIND
DIRECTION

PERIMETER REINFORCED
CONCRETE PUNCHED
WALL SYSTEM

WIND
DIRECTION

HIGH FORCE (TENSION)
LOW FORCE (T/C)
HIGH FORCE (COMPRESSION)

AL SYSTEM CONCEPT   WIND DEFLECTION DIAGRAM   PERIMETER PUNCHED WALL WIND AXIAL FORCE DIAGRAMS

UNDEFORMED
SHAPE

DEFORMED
SHAPE (30x)

WIND
DIRECTION

WIND
DIRECTION

PERIMETER REINFORCED
CONCRETE PUNCHED
WALL SYSTEM

WIND
DIRECTION

HIGH FORCE (TENSION)
LOW FORCE (T/C)
HIGH FORCE (COMPRESSION)

tructural studies

ollowing pages:
eft: Floor plans and cross section
ight: Photocollage of building and site

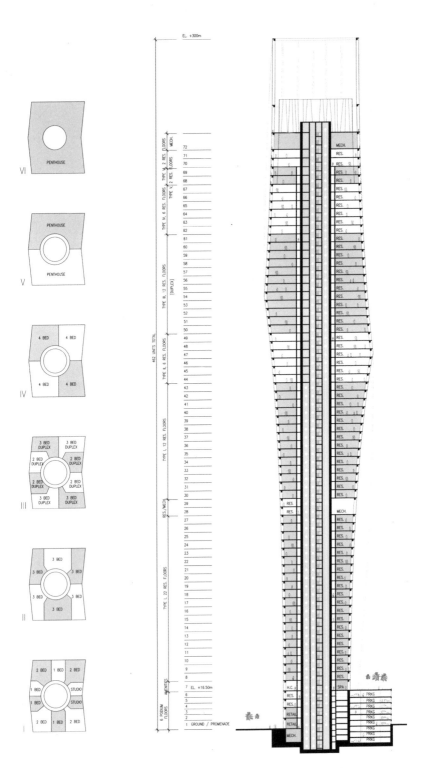

BUILDING SECTION

Perspective rendering of top of building

Jordan Mozer and Associates

East Hotel, Hamburg, Germany, 2005

Occupying what was once a dilapidated, abandoned iron foundry, the hotel East is now a radiant new gem in the increasingly popular St. Pauli district of Hamburg, Germany. To transform an industrial ruin into a sophisticated hot spot, Jordan Mozer and Associates developed a two-structure complex around a central garden courtyard, using the shell of the old foundry to house the main entrance, all dining and entertainment areas, and twelve special guest rooms, while creating an entirely new building for the main hotel rooms and parking. More than just a structural renovation, however, East Hotel also presents a dazzling interior built around a 250-seat restaurant with 35-foot ceilings and four sets of 28-foot-tall glass doors. At the cellar level the restaurant offers intimate dining spaces carved into the original brickwork of the foundry, while on the main level Colours Lounge and Yakshi's Bar flank the triple-height volume of the restaurant. The elegant Smirnoff Lounge 3 skybox overlooks the dining area from the second floor.

Original furniture and designed objects throughout East exemplify Mozer's other talents. Inspired by the ghosts of the old foundry, these elements honor the building's history, while introducing a contemporary, Asian-influenced flair. Components were cast in bronze, resin, plaster, and magnesium aluminum alloy, and while their shapes reflect cooled molten slag, their progressive designs suggest an overall modern fluidity.

View of hotel room

Following pages:
View of restaurant

View of Smirnoff Lounge 3

View of Colours Lounge

Holly Hunt

South Beach Chair, 2004 Studio H Collection
Chantacaille Lamp, Christian Liaigre at Holly Hunt, 2004
Barbuda Chair, Christian Liaigre at Holly Hunt, 1997

Revered in the home furnishings and interior design industries, Holly Hunt has developed a reputation for products offering crisp sophistication, modern elegance, and everyday comfort. Graduating with degrees in literature and the design of clothing and textiles, Hunt initially aspired to become a fashion designer. In 1984, however, she found her place in the furniture industry. She showcased leading designers in her establishments for nearly ten years before creating the Holly Hunt Collection of Furniture in 1993. Today she operates showrooms in Chicago, Los Angeles, Miami, Minneapolis, New York City, and Washington, D.C. Renowned for her business savvy, Hunt brings accomplished talent—such as the well-known European designer Christian Liaigre—under the Holly Hunt Collection name. With this strategy, Liaigre's high-end couture furnishings are now available to a larger audience.

As seen in their custom chair designs, both Hunt and Liaigre create classic modern, streamlined pieces. Both utilize dark wood and clean lines to enhance an abstract, minimalist feel. Each piece, however, suggests a different historic period in design. Reminiscent of a bar chair, Hunt's piece touts curvilinear lines, while Liaigre produces an object that reflects the eighteenth-century wing chair. Hunt brings the same contemporary austerity to her design of a floor lamp.

South Beach Chair

Chantacaille Lamp, Christian Liaigre at Holly Hunt

Barbuda Chair, Christian Liaigre at Holly Hunt

Motorola

Audex Jacket, with Burton Snowboards, 2006
SLVR, 2006
RAZR, 2006
Moto Q, 2006
PEBL, 2006

A Chicago-based company known for its cutting-edge industrial design and technology, Motorola was established as the Galvin Manufacturing Corporation in 1928. The company first produced the battery eliminator—a device enabling battery-powered radios to run on standard household current. Founder Paul V. Galvin created the brand name "Motorola" in 1930 for the company's new car radio, linking *motor* (motorcar) with the suffix *ola* (Victrola). Six years later, the company launched its Motorola Police Cruiser mobile receiver—a redesigned car radio preset to a single frequency to receive police broadcasts—the firm's first entry into the new field of mobile radio communications.

While consumers have linked the Motorola brand to televisions since the late 1940s, today's buyers more readily identify the company with the booming cellular phone industry. This evolution is best seen in the company's fresh marketing campaign, targeting the skateboard generation and young professionals. Motorola sells not only cellular products but also the lifestyles that accompany them, offering a variety of design styles and colors to match select demographics. With the PEBL, RAZR, and SLVR phones, Motorola's designs have become iconic for the technically savvy and stylish younger generation. To reach their target audience even further, Motorola has partnered with other companies such as Burton Snowboards to create popular hybrid products, highlighting the best each company has to offer. The Burton Audex jacket features Motorola's state-of-the-art audio in a fashionable cargo for trendsetters on the move.

Audex jacket, with Burton Snowboards

Following pages:
Above left: SLVR
Below left: RAZR
Above right: Moto Q
Below right: PEBL

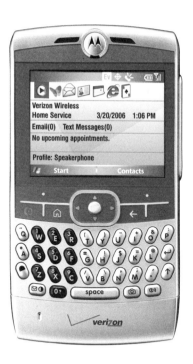

IDEO

Altec Lansing, inMotion iM7, 2005
Organ Recovery Systems, LifePort Kidney Transporter, 2004
Eli Lilly and Co., Humatrope Reconstitution Device, 2005

IDEO helps companies create products, services, environments, and digital experiences. Its innovative studios employ world-class teams that together examine a product's desirability, technical feasibility, and financial viability. Focusing on a user's or consumer's potential experience with a given product, IDEO designers explore such aspects as seeing, desiring, obtaining, and using a product, while integrating business, human, and technical factors into its creation. Their talent lies in the ability to fashion pleasing aesthetic forms that fulfill a product's stated purpose.

IDEO assisted Organ Recovery Systems in the production of the LifePort Kidney Transporter, a technically advanced alternative to the traditional form of kidney transport—a cooler filled with ice. This new device gently pumps the organ with a cold liquid solution, while its user interface presents essential information, and its compact, ergonomic design respects the needs of those transporting and transplanting vital cargo. The Humatrope Reconstitution Device created for Eli Lilly and Co.—awarded the 2005 Medical Design Excellence Award—exemplifies IDEO's sense of streamlined efficiency. Used in the treatment of growth hormone deficiencies, this instrument eliminates the multistep process of mixing powder and liquid and enables parents to administer an injection at home to children aged six to eighteen. The syringe is encased in a glass outer shell; the side-firing tip indirectly spills the already encased liquid into the powder, preventing unwanted foaming; the recessed needle stops accidental sticks; and a protective cap enables users to dispose of the device securely.

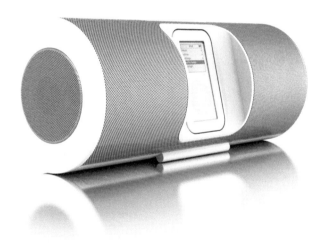

Altec Lansing, inMotion iM7

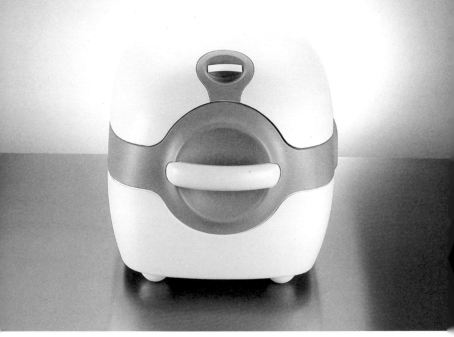

Top, top right, and above: Organ Recovery Systems,
LifePort Kidney Transporter
Above right: Eli Lilly and Co., Humatrope Reconstitution Device

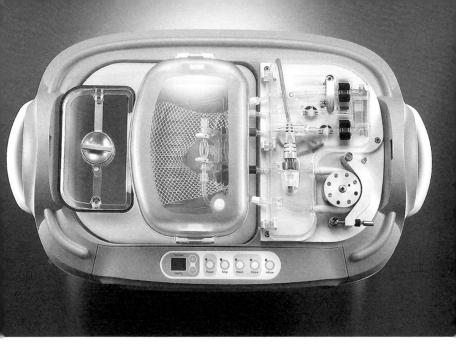

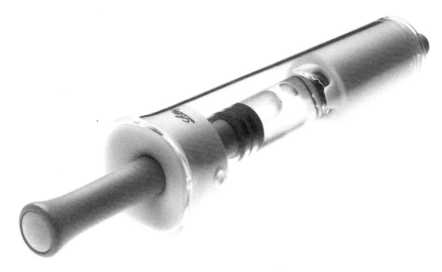

Studio Blue

Ford Calumet Environmental Center, design competition entry, 2004
Otis College of Art and Design, brand identity and catalogue design, 2003
Studio Gang/O'Donnell, graphic identity system, 2001
Harry N. Abrams, Inc., Marcel Duchamp: The Art of Making Art in the Age of Mechanical Reproduction, book design, 1999

"Making artifacts that matter" is the impetus behind the graphic designs at Studio Blue. Founded in 1993 by Cheryl Towler Weese, the studio was soon joined by Kathy Fredrickson. Early on the partners devoted themselves to cultural and educational institutions—the Chicago Historical Society, Field Museum, and Chicago Architecture Foundation, to name but a few—creating printed materials, books, exhibits, signage systems, identities, and Web sites. Each of their projects demonstrates the firm's self-described "obsessive sensitivity" to typographical nuances, as well as their commitment to in-depth research and collaborative teamwork.

To create a catalogue for the Otis College of Art and Design, the Studio Blue team immersed themselves in the culture of the school and its students, while also examining teen magazines and student blogs to identify age-specific language and interests. The result of their research produced a vibrant color palette reflecting the energy and climate of this Southern California institution, offered up in the language of "splats," a symbolic commentary on the art-making process. For the book *Marcel Duchamp: The Art of Making Art in the Age of Mechanical Reproduction*, they created a typographical treatment, layout, and composition exhibiting a crisp modern minimalism with historic reference. Honoring Duchamp's own interest in typography and optics, Studio Blue fashioned the front cover after a Russian eye chart that Duchamp owned. The use and placement of classic modern typography is inventively explored in their new identity system for Studio Gang/O'Donnell, a Chicago architecture firm.

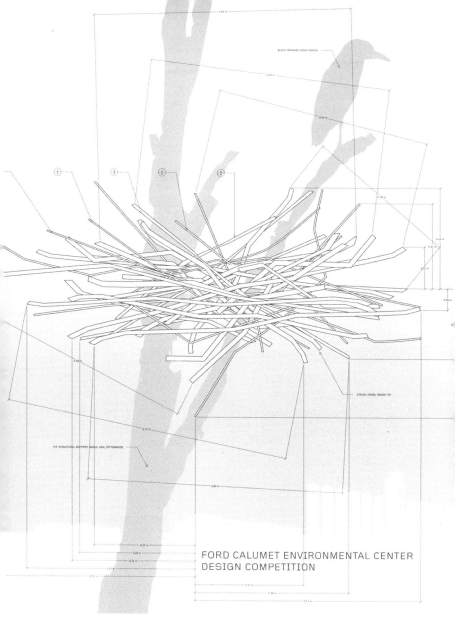

BLACK CROWNED NIGHT HERON

STICKS, TWIGS, REEDS TYP.

TYP. STRUCTURAL SUPPORT, MAPLE, ASH, COTTONWOOD

FORD CALUMET ENVIRONMENTAL CENTER
DESIGN COMPETITION

Ford Calumet Environmental Center, design competition entry

Otis College of Art and Design, brand identity and
catalogue design

STUDIO
GANG/
O'DONNELL

STU
GAN
O'DO

ARCHITECTURE
LANDSCAPE
URBAN DESIGN

3656 N. LINCOLN AVE
UNIT G
CHICAGO, IL 60613

STUDIO@STUDIO
GANGODONNELL.COM

T 773 929 7974
F 773 929 7254

UDIO
NG/
ONNELL

STUDIO
GANG/
O'DONNELL

STUDIO

STUDIO
GANG/
O'DONNELL

ARCHITECTURE
LANDSCAPE
URBAN DESIGN

JUNKO GOSEKI

3656 N. LINCOLN AVE
UNIT G
CHICAGO, IL 60613
T 773 929 7974
F 773 929 7254

STUDIO

KODONNELL@STUDIOGANGODONNELL.COM

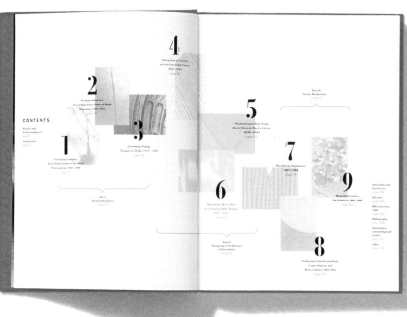

Above: Harry N. Abrams, Inc., *Marcel Duchamp: The Art of Making Art in the Age of Mechanical Reproduction*, book design
Left: Studio Gang/O'Donnell, graphic identity system

JNL Graphic Design

Avec, graphic identity system, 2005
The Aluminum Group, Happyness, CD packaging, 2003
University of Illinois at Chicago, School of Architecture, graphic
identity system, 2005

After a four-year apprenticeship with the highly esteemed Chicago graphic
designer Michael Glass, Jason Pickleman created JNL Graphic Design in
1992 with his wife, Leslie Bodenstein. Specializing in "graphics of cultural
significance," JNL Graphic Design counts among its clients architects, cura-
tors and museums, entrepreneurs, fashion designers, and others in the
PR and magazine industries. Pickleman produces catalogues, identities,
and advertising, in addition to a variety of ancillary materials.

While many graphic designers seek perfection in their work, JNL Design successfully explores the beauty of flaws and imperfections. This
celebration of error is masterfully displayed in Pickleman's creative work
for the Chicago restaurant Avec. As evident on the cover of the restaurant's
menu, all typography is struck through in a glorious repetition of editorial
practice, while the typesetting of the restaurant's name, avec, is power-
fully revealed. Another example of Pickleman's playfulness with standards
of perfection is his packaging for the Aluminum Group's CD *Happyness*.
While many might consider a portrait with three mouths and five eyes a
woeful photographic mishap or graphic design lapse, Pickleman's frag-
mented, multiple images imply rollicking movement. His bold sense of
style is displayed again in the identity system he created for the School of
Architecture at the University of Illinois at Chicago. Here traditional word
breaks are entirely discarded in favor of the overall graphic composition.

Avec, graphic identity system

THE
ALUMINUM
GROUP
"HAPPYNESS"

The Aluminum Group, *Happyness*, CD packaging

Following pages:
University of Illinois at Chicago, School of Architecture,
graphic identity system

ARE

RE

VIEW

@UIC

REFRESHER
COURSE FOR THE
ARCHITECT
REGISTRATION
EXAM

MAY 25 –
AUGUST 12
2004

UIC University of Illinois at Chicago

SCHOOL
OF
ARCHITEC
TURE

02.02

MONDAY, FEBRUARY 2

"MODERNIST OPPORTUNITIES"

ELLEN DINEEN GRIMES

University of Illinois at Chicago

02.16

MONDAY, FEBRUARY 16

"LEGIBILITY + RESILIENCE"

JULIA CZER NIAK

Syracuse University
Co-sponsored by Chicago Women in Architecture

03.09

TUESDAY, MARCH 9

"BEAT SCIENCE"

SAN FORD KWIN TER

Rice University
Co-sponsored by the Graham Foundation for Advanced Studies in the Fine Arts; and the Architecture and Design Society, The Art Institute of Chicago

SPECIAL LOCATION:
Price Auditorium, The Art Institute of Chicago (Michigan Avenue entrance, lower level)

04.19

MONDAY, APRIL 19

"METALLICA"

KIEL MOE

University of Illinois at Chicago
2004 Greenwald Visiting Critic

03.29

MONDAY, MARCH 29

"TOPOGRAPHIES OF PRAXIS"

DAVID LEATH ERBAR ROW

University of Pennsylvania
Co-sponsored by A3, the UIC Architecture Alumni Association

Fold Four

New Art Publications, BOMB, magazine design, 2006
Whitney Museum of American Art, Rob Fischer, exhibition brochure, 2005
Whitney Museum of American Art, Andrea Zittel, invitation, 2005
Clogs, Lantern, CD packaging, 2005

Unconventional thinking and a rigorous pursuit of typographical refinement and expression are Roy Brooks's hallmarks. As an architecture student at North Carolina State University, Brooks realized his relative indifference to the program when he discovered that his creativity was in fact ignited by the energy and challenges of the university's graphic design department. Upon earning his bachelor's degree in 1997, Brooks began his professional relationship with cultural institutions by working as a designer at the Whitney Museum of American Art in New York. Later, as an employee of Pentagram, he worked on a variety of projects for the Guggenheim Museum, the Rock and Roll Hall of Fame and Museum, and the Dallas Museum of Art. In 2005 Brooks followed his entrepreneurial spirit by founding Fold Four design in Chicago. His current clients include *BOMB* magazine, Chronicle Books, the Whitney Museum, and the Art Institute of Chicago.

A defining characteristic of *BOMB* is Brooks's ability to blur the traditional boundaries of graphic layout. By selecting a classic book grid for a magazine, Brooks offers an atypical experience for his readers, forcing them to question their interaction with the publication. His innovative composition can also be found in his brochure for a Whitney Museum exhibition on artist Rob Fischer. By wrapping images and text continually over the surface, Brooks delightfully engages the reader in extended handling and exploration of the piece. The theme of a visual continuum is also seen in Brooks's treatment of an invitation for another Whitney show on Andrea Zittel.

BOMB, magazine design, 2006, original template designed
with Matt Peterson while at Field Study
Following pages: Whitney Museum of American Art,
Rob Fischer, exhibition brochure

→ I bet you that this song is about you, 2005. Steel, mirror, and paint, 54 × 93 × 276 in. (137 × 236 × 701 cm). Courtesy Cohen and Leslie, New York

↑ left view of installation

The door for life stands on 2005. Wood stars, 54

→ Living Will, 2005. Wood, plaster, light, and wiring, 72 × 96 × 30 in. (183 × 244 × 76 cm). Courtesy Cohen and Leslie, New York

→ Manyfold (Westfaul) 2005. Wood and steel, 86 × 86 × 78 in. (218 × 218 × 198 cm). Courtesy Cohen and Leslie, New York

→ Not waving but drowning, 2005. Fiberglass boat, steel, mirrors, wiring, lights, and construction adhesive, 90 × 56 × 46 in. (229 × 142 × 117 cm). Courtesy Cohen and Leslie, New York

→ Not waving but drowning, 2005. Fiberglass boat, steel, mirrors, wiring, lights, and construction adhesive, 90 × 56 × 46 in. (229 × 142 × 117 cm). Courtesy Cohen and Leslie, New York

ROB FISCHER

Your vigor for life expells me, 2005. Wood, plaster, lights, wiring, plumbing, flooring and scaffolding, 288 × 288 × 420 in. (732 × 732 × 1,067 cm). Courtesy Cohan and Leslie, New York, and Mary Goldman Gallery, Los Angeles

WHITNEY Whitney Museum of American Art at Altria

30 Yards (Minor Tragedies Dissected), 2005. Steel, glass, cherry, roadsalt, pickup truck bed, fuselage, tractor, pipes, electrical conduit, wiring, lights, fan, wood, plywood, wood flooring papers, and paint, 60¼ × 156 × 172 in. (154 × 396 × 437 cm). Courtesy Cohan and Leslie, New York, and Mary Goldman Gallery, Los Angeles

ROB FISCHER:
Here Is Always Somewhere Else

Men dream of flying because they thirst for a state of mind where
they need not worry about the placement of their feet.
Robert Grossman, *The Book of Lazarus*[1]

That's the problem, I thought—most people try to tell the many
stories of their lives but are interrupted, time and again, until they
begin to forget them.

Gina Ochsner, *People I Wanted to Be*[2]

HOW DO WE EXPLAIN A LIFE, OUR OWN or any individual's? "How did I end up here?" These are questions that we tend to want to answer by citing a series of singular events—things that either happened to us or that were precipitated by us, a good story unfurled as a narrative of critical choices and dramatic moments that have shifted and diverted our paths according to a clear vision of who and what we would become. But in fact the trajectories are not as magisterial as we would like to believe: it is usually the minute, unnoticed decisions that shape our existence, and those are much harder to track. Failed or successful attempts to fulfill our desires require continued renegotiation and reorientation, and follow a far more elliptical, regenerative cycle than the teleological linearity of a cause-and-effect narrative. Perhaps the things that one strives to *not* be are in fact the most present, existing quietly behind those attempts toward grandeur. To further complicate things, life's stories are often swayed by our motivations to retell and make better sense of "the way it was."

Throughout his earlier practice, and most explicitly in recent sculptural installations he describes as "footnotes to an unknown story,"[3] Brooklyn-based artist Rob Fischer addresses the revisions of these contingent, aleatory histories. Fischer's sculptures have often incorporated recycled

vehicle parts or vernacular architectural elements familiar to the landscape of his native Minnesota—trailers, boats, single-room cabins and houses, trucks, Dumpsters—for their formal and material qualities as well as the individual stories embedded in their histories. It is easy to imagine that the spatial relationships of the layered sculptural forms and our path through and among them (which becomes of increasing importance in his work) might suggest a diary of use. However, rather than functioning as an explicit series of true events, for Fischer the forms are cartographic, mapping specifics and deeply linked to a lived reality while also abstracted to a set of symbols that have broader and more universal meaning.

In Fischer's most recent large-scale installation of works from 2005 at the Whitney Museum at Altria, it is perhaps the smallest work—a diptych of photographs—that anchors and illuminates his media and practice. In *Highway 71 (Blur)* the two snapshot-like images of a group of parked trucks in an anonymous American countryside have clearly been taken from inside a moving vehicle. The setting sun glints on the edge of a car window, its glare challenged by a bright orange of trucks bursting into flames beyond—the color painted on the image by the artist. The blurring of the

Whitney Museum of American Art, Andrea Zittel, invitation

ANDREA ZITTEL

WEDNESDAY, FEBRUARY 8, 2006, 7–9 PM
WHITNEY MUSEUM OF AMERICAN ART
AT ALTRIA

120 PARK AVENUE AT 42ND STREET

ADMISSION IS BY INVITATION ONLY. THIS INVITATION ADMITS TWO.

SMALL LIBERTIES

Nick Cave

Soundsuit, 2006

In 1993 fiber artist Nick Cave cofounded the successful Chicago fashion
and design company Robave, Inc. He quickly became known for producing
timeless garments, created from elegant and luxurious fabrics with the
finest detailing. Every decision regarding fabric, color, surface design,
shape, and cut was carefully considered. Currently devoted to visual and
performance art, Cave explores and redefines the cultural and conceptual connotations of textiles and clothing as an extension of the body.
Through *Soundsuits*, the African-American artist draws upon his cultural
heritage to express social issues. The suits emerge as static sculptures for
exhibition, as well as ritualistic costumes for performance, while thought-
fully engaging in social commentary. *Soundsuits* provide protection and
disguise against the prejudices that minorities endure in this country.
Purposefully, *Soundsuits* are made from found materials of little value, a
characteristic that the designer believes reflects society's interpretation
of the black male in America. Likened to ceremonial costumes in various
cultures, Cave's *Soundsuits* transform the individual under the shield of
anonymity, encouraging experimental motion and spontaneous experiences. Each suit—composed of different materials—produces a unique
sound as the wearer moves. In this regard, the garment becomes muse to
the wearer during artistic performances.

Soundsuit

Cat Chow

Hourglass, 2003

The intriguing quality of Cat Chow's work begins with her ability to step beyond the conventional use of materials. Her fascination with nontraditional methods of fabrication developed while she was a theater major at Northwestern University. In her freshman year she worked at a costume shop, where the flexible metal-ring mesh of chain mail captivated her. She once envisioned a wearable garment composed of this archaic material. Having expanded her inventive perspective on unusual materials, Chow now transforms everyday objects—twist ties, tissues, corks, or zippers—into elegant gowns or imaginative pieces of installation art.

While Cat Chow's incomparable fabrications propel fashion design forward, her work reflects the fine craftsmanship of a traditional couturier. During her years studying theatrical costume design as an undergraduate, she took courses in pattern making and clothing construction. Her skills now enable her to manipulate fabric so that it retains her careful positioning of it, whether the piece is worn or placed on display. In *Hourglass*, Chow's design and construction captures the essence and beauty of the female form—without a physical body. By altering the perspective of the garment, the piece becomes a work of sculptural art. Inspired by artists Tom Friedman and Donald Lipski—sculptors who use unexpected materials—Chow blurs the boundary between fashion and fine art.

Hourglass

Biographies

Qua'Virarch

Paul Preissner founded the architectural office Qua'Virarch in 2003 in Los Angeles and relocated to Chicago in 2004. He received his MArch from Columbia University and worked for Eisenman Architects; Skidmore, Owings & Merrill; and Wood + Zapata. He currently teaches at the University of Illinois at Chicago and is the Visiting Hyde Chair at the University of Nebraska — Lincoln.

UrbanLab

Sarah Dunn and Martin Felsen met while pursuing their master's degrees at Columbia University, and established their own architecture studio, UrbanLab, in 2000. Dunn worked for OMA in Rotterdam and led the project team for the Illinois Institute of Technology McCormick Tribune Campus Center. She also teaches at the University of Illinois at Chicago. Felsen worked for Stan Allen Architect before moving to Chicago to teach at IIT.

Clare Lyster Studio

After receiving her BArch from University College Dublin and her MArch from Yale University, Clare Lyster worked in the New York offices of Thomas Hanrahan + Victoria Meyers Architects and Matthew Baird Design. In 2001 she moved to Chicago when she was awarded the Alvin Boyarsky Research Fellowship at the University of Illinois at Chicago; she continues to teach, write, and research issues pertaining to the production of contemporary public space while running a small design studio.

3D Design Studio

Architects Melinda Palmore and Darryl Crosby met during architecture school at the University of Illinois at Chicago, formed a partnership in 1995, and began their own firm, 3D Design Studio, in 1997. 3D Design Studio has completed designs for numerous competitions and built work in and around Chicago. Both Palmore and Crosby teach architecture- and design-related courses at Columbia College.

Avram Lothan, DeStefano + Partners

Avram Lothan, FAIA, LEED AP, is design principal at DeStefano + Partners, Ltd., an architecture, urban planning, and interior design firm with offices in Chicago and Los Angeles. Lothan received his MArch from Harvard University and has worked at DeStefano since 1990. He has also taught at the University of Illinois at Chicago and Harvard's Graduate School of Design.

John Ronan Architect

John Ronan graduated with an MArch with distinction from Harvard University's Graduate School of Design. He worked in the offices of Tigerman Fugman McCurry and Krueck and Sexton before starting his own firm in 1997. Since that time, the firm's work has won several design competitions and appeared in numerous international publications. Ronan is also an assistant professor at the Illinois Institute of Technology.

Ross B. Wimer, Skidmore, Owings & Merrill

Ross B. Wimer is a design partner at Skidmore, Owings & Merrill LLP, an international architecture, interior design, urban planning, and engineering firm that was founded in Chicago in 1936. He received his BA from Yale University and his MArch from Harvard University and began at SOM in 1995. In addition to serving as lead architect on several SOM projects, Wimer has served on numerous competition and fellowship juries.

Jordan Mozer and Associates

Designer Jordan Mozer founded the interdisciplinary architecture, product, and design firm Jordan Mozer and Associates, Ltd. (JMA) in Chicago in 1984. Jeff Carloss, partner, began working at JMA in 1992, adding to the team's experience with restaurant and hospitality design. Partner Tom Rossiter, FAIA, recently joined JMA after serving as managing director of AECOM Facilities and president of McClier.

Holly Hunt

After obtaining degrees in English and clothing/textile design, Holly Hunt moved to Chicago to begin working as a fashion designer. During the mid-1980s, however, she decided to switch to designing furniture and thus embarked on a new career path. Hunt's first store opened in Chicago in 1984; she now has storefronts in Los Angeles, Miami, Minneapolis, New York, and Washington, D.C.

Motorola

Founded as Galvin Manufacturing Company in 1928, Motorola specializes in the design and manufacture of electronic and mobile communication devices, from car radios and walkie-talkies to televisions and cellular phones. Peter Pfanner is the director of Global Design Integration at Motorola, headquartered in suburban Chicago. He has over fifteen years of experience as a designer and consultant at organizations such as IDEO, Pentagram, and HFID.

IDEO

IDEO, a multidisciplinary design consultancy, was founded in Palo Alto, California, in 1991, and has since expanded to include offices in Boston, Chicago, and San Francisco, as well as London, Munich, and Shanghai. Their design strategy involves teams of specialists from many different fields who work together to brainstorm solutions for all aspects of a product's design and manufacturing. Martin Thaler is the design studio lead for the Chicago office.

Studio Blue

Cheryl Towler Weese established Studio Blue in 1993 after receiving her MFA in graphic design from Yale University. She was joined a year later by Kathy Fredrickson, who earned her MA from the School of the Art Institute of Chicago and had been working at the Art Institute as the associate director of publications in charge of production. Their full-service graphic design studio now has a total of eight team members.

JNL Graphic Design

Jason Pickleman is a self-taught artist and graphic designer whose studio, JNL Graphic Design, bridges the gap between fine and commercial art. After obtaining a bachelor's degree in English literature, Pickleman completed a four-year apprenticeship under noted designer Michael Glass and started his own studio shortly thereafter. JNL Graphic Design has produced exhibition catalogs, public art, and "informational propaganda" for a number of high-profile clients.

Fold Four

Roy Brooks's solo graphic design practice, Fold Four, was founded in 2005. After graduating from North Carolina State University with a degree in graphic design, Brooks moved to New York City, where he worked as a designer at the Whitney Museum of American Art and at Pentagram. In 2002 he moved to Chicago and started the design studio Field Study with former classmate Matthew Peterson; this partnership was dissolved when Peterson returned to North Carolina.

Nick Cave

Nick Cave is an interdisciplinary artist, working within and beyond the fields of sculpture, performance, installation, and dance. He received his MFA from the Cranbrook Academy of Art. In addition to teaching studio courses as a tenured faculty member and chair of the Department of Fashion Design at the School of the Art Institute of Chicago, Cave has also produced work for over 200 exhibitions.

Cat Chow

Fashion designer and artist Cat Chow received her Bachelor of Science in theater, with an emphasis on costume design, from Northwestern University. She started her solo practice in 1996 and has since participated in dozens of exhibitions and won several awards, including the Louis Comfort Tiffany Biennial Award in 2003. Her *Bonded (Zipper) Dress* has been acquired by the Metropolitan Museum of Art.